Girls Who Choose God

STORIES OF EXTRAORDINARY WOMEN FROM CHURCH HISTORY

McARTHUR KRISHNA • BETHANY BRADY SPALDING

ILLUSTRATED BY KATHLEEN PETERSON

DESERET BOOK

Salt Lake City, Utah

*To the truly extraordinary Laird Ladies, who taught me that Mormon women
can be faithful and feisty! Alisa Allred Mercer, Annie Hinckley Stucki,
Jessie Lorimer, Johanna Buchert Smith, Tiffany Ivins Spence, and
the many others who joined in the Laird love along the way.*
—BBS

To my mom, whose unwavering trust in God inspires me every day.
—MK

To my sweet Stella, Nina, and Cece.
—KP

Text © 2019 McArthur Krishna and Bethany Brady Spalding

Illustrations © 2019 Kathleen Peterson

Art direction by Richard Erickson
Design by Shauna Gibby

Library of Congress Cataloging-in-Publication Data
Names: Krishna, McArthur, author. | Spalding, Bethany Brady, author. | Illustrator. Peterson, Kathleen, 1951–
Title: Girls who choose God : stories of extraordinary women from church history / McArthur Krishna and Bethany Brady Spalding ; illustrated by Kathleen Peterson.
Description: Salt Lake City, Utah : Deseret Book, 2019. | Includes bibliographical references.
Identifiers: LCCN 2019019839 | ISBN 9781629726274 (hardbound : alk. paper)
Subjects: LCSH: Mormon women—Biography—Juvenile literature.
Classification: LCC BX8693 .K75 2019 | DDC 289.3092/52 [B] —dc23
LC record available at https://lccn.loc.gov/2019019839

Printed in China   06/2019
Four Colour Print Group, Nansha, China

10 9 8 7 6 5 4 3 2 1

INTRODUCTION

"My dear sisters, you have special spiritual gifts and propensities. . . . I urge you, with all the hope of my heart, to pray to understand your spiritual gifts—to cultivate, use, and expand them, even more than you ever have. You will change the world as you do so."

—President Russell M. Nelson

These fifteen women from our early Church history were extraordinary! Drawing on their deep faith and embracing their unique spiritual gifts, they made choices that changed their families, their communities, the Church, and the course of generations to come. God's goodness shined through these women, and we hope that you are enlightened by their stories.

This book does not attempt to be a comprehensive biography of these women's incredible, colorful, complex lives. Rather, we have highlighted a moment of choice when their decision to choose God had profound impact. We are immensely grateful for the brilliant Church historians whose knowledge and expertise made this collection possible: Jill Derr, Kate Holbrook, Brittany Chapman Nash, Jenny Reeder, Lisa Olsen Tait, and Mark Staker.

May these extraordinary women inspire us to choose God in our everyday lives.

Bethany and McArthur

LUCY MACK SMITH
Mother Moses

Lucy was a believer. She had always believed her son Joseph as he taught about a loving God and founded a new church. Now the Church was growing and the Saints needed to gather together to build their faith. It was time for Lucy to put her belief into action. She was elected the leader of a group of eighty women, men, and children moving more than 250 miles from Fayette, New York, to Kirtland, Ohio. Traveling by boat was a challenge, and the group was often wet, hungry, and cold. Lucy did all she could to lead and care for her people. But one frigid day, Buffalo Harbor froze over and every boat was trapped. The Saints were stuck! Many people started complaining.

Lucy had a choice to make. She could feel that God had forgotten them,

or

she could believe that a loving God would provide a way.

Lucy chose to believe. Her soul was filled with fervent faith. She believed that no matter what, God could help her people—and she reminded everyone who forgot:

"Where is your faith? Where is your confidence in God? . . . Now, brethren and sisters, if you will all of you raise your desires to heaven, that the ice may be broken up, and we be set at liberty, as sure as the Lord lives, it will be done."

Right as Lucy spoke, there was a thunderous crack! The ice miraculously parted and let only the boat Lucy was leading pass through before freezing closed again. Sailing safely on their way, Lucy and her people united with the other Saints in Kirtland. Lucy's faith had inspired her people to believe, and a loving God blessed them with a miracle. Just as in Moses's day, the waters had parted and Lucy led her people to the promised land. Hallelujah!

When have you chosen to believe that God will help you?

Emma Hale Smith
An Extraordinary Leader

Emma was extraordinary. She had the courage and conviction to do things that hadn't been done before. Against many obstacles, Emma worked closely with her husband, Joseph, to build The Church of Jesus Christ of Latter-day Saints. God told Emma that she had been specially chosen to be a leader in the Church. In a revelation, God asked her to teach and encourage the Saints by explaining the scriptures and sharing sacred songs. Emma was surprised by this calling, because in her time, it was unusual for women to lead.

❖

Emma had a choice to make. She could do what was ordinary,

or

she could become the leader God knew she could be.

Emma chose to lead. She declared, "We are going to do something extraordinary!" With great enthusiasm, Emma taught truths to the members of the Church. She worked as a scribe during the translation of the Book of Mormon. She created the first Church hymnbook and led the Saints in lifting their voices to God. As the first President of the Relief Society, Emma built unity among a diverse group of women and urged the Saints to care for the poor. She always led by example—compassionately welcoming strangers into her home, caring for the sick, adopting orphans, and feeding the hungry. Emma was truly extraordinary!

———◇———

When have you chosen to be extraordinary?

Mary Elizabeth and Caroline Rollins

The Revelation Rescuers

Mary Elizabeth and Caroline were daring! The sisters lived in a thrilling time in Independence, Missouri, in 1833. God was speaking to the Saints, and the Prophet Joseph was compiling these revelations into a book. The sisters were only teenagers, but they were eager to learn new truths from God. The revelations were revolutionary! They taught Mary Elizabeth and Caroline that they were children of Heavenly Parents who knew them by name. The Rollins sisters were excited that a press was printing copies of the book.

One day Mary Elizabeth and Caroline saw a mean mob breaking into the printing shop, throwing pages of the book into the dirt yard, and smashing the press. The sisters knew the printed revelations were in danger of being destroyed.

⟳━━━━◆━━━━⟲

Mary Elizabeth and Caroline had a choice to make. They could run away to safety,

or

they could try to save the revelations.

The sisters chose to be daring. They ran toward the printing shop, picked up as many pages as they could, and raced to a nearby cornfield to hide. Mary Elizabeth and Caroline covered the pages with their bodies and buried their heads, praying not to be found. As the men walked up and down the rows of corn, hunting for them, the shivering girls tried to stay still. The mob came within a few feet of where the girls were lying. Desperately, the sisters kept praying—and God protected them. The sisters were not found! Finally, the men gave up and left. Mary Elizabeth and Caroline had helped save the revelations!

When have you dared to do what is right?

ELIZA R. SNOW
Zion's Poetess

Eliza was a poet. She began writing as a young girl about her favorite subjects of history, politics, and patriotism. By the age of twenty-two, Eliza had become very popular in her home state of Ohio. She was even asked by a local newspaper to publish a poem about two presidents of the United States. With boundless talent, Eliza was on her way to worldly success. But when she was thirty-one, she discovered the gospel and was invited to join a group of humble Saints in Kirtland.

❦

Eliza had a choice to make. She could write poems in hopes of fame and fortune,

or

she could use her poetry to inspire simple seekers of truth.

Eliza chose to devote her poetry to inspiring the Saints. With the stroke of her pen, she taught many heavenly truths to the people of Kirtland and Nauvoo. Eliza also became the teacher to Joseph and Emma Smith's family. In her lifetime, Eliza wrote over five hundred poems. One of her most loved poems was "Invocation, or the Eternal Father and Mother," celebrating the restored truth of Heavenly Parents. Speaking at the October 1893 general conference, the prophet Wilford Woodruff called Eliza's poem a revelation. She wrote:

"In the heav'ns are parents single? No, the thought makes reason stare! Truth is reason; truth eternal tells me I've a mother there."

Eliza never was a mother herself, but she loved writing poems for Primary children's songs and lessons. Eliza kept writing and writing—even during her decades as Relief Society General President. Spreading beauty and truth to all, Eliza became known as Zion's Poetess.

———◆———

When have you chosen to put God first?

ZINA YOUNG
The Great Mother Heart

Zina had a big heart. As a young girl, she loved to help her family, friends, and even strangers. Zina was gentle, quiet, and caring. Shortly after Zina was baptized at the age of fourteen, she received a powerful spiritual gift. All of a sudden, this soft-spoken girl had the gift of tongues and could speak and understand many languages. The gift was so unusual that Zina was afraid to use it. As she hid her spiritual gift, it began to fade until it was almost lost. Zina's heart was sad.

Zina had a choice to make. She could fear her spiritual gift and let it fade away,

or

she could claim her gift and use it for good.

Zina chose to use her spiritual gift. But she didn't know quite what to do—so she asked her mother. Zina's wise mother encouraged her to turn to God in prayer. Listening to her mother, Zina walked down to a little spring in a lovely meadow and prayed with her whole heart. She humbly asked God for forgiveness and to please restore her gift. Zina promised that whenever she was prompted, she would use it "no matter where or when."

God heard Zina's prayers and restored the gift of tongues. After Zina embraced her gift, God poured out many more spiritual gifts upon her. Zina ministered to countless Saints in need of healing. She was a blessing to women during childbirth, and she also brought comfort and radiance to the sick and the dying. Using her spiritual gifts to bless others, Zina became known as the Great Mother Heart.

———◆———

When have you used your spiritual gifts to bless others?

Jane Manning James
The Unstoppable Pioneer

Jane was unstoppable. When she heard missionaries preach in Connecticut, she "was fully convinced that it was the true Gospel." Jane was baptized in the 1840s, making her one of the first African Americans to join the Church.

Jane had a burning desire to gather with the Saints, and she would not give up until she did. She tried to catch a boat to get to Nauvoo, but the captain stole her money and refused to take her. Jane was often discriminated against because of the color of her skin, but that didn't stop her. Jane just started walking. Along the way, her luggage was lost and people threatened to put her in jail, but Jane didn't give up. Her shoes were worn out, and her feet became sore and cracked open and bled—but she didn't stop. Walking over eight hundred grueling miles, Jane led her family and friends to join the Saints. The Prophet Joseph and Emma Smith were inspired by Jane, and they became dear friends. After Joseph's death, the Saints were asked to gather in a new place—this time in the mountains and deserts of the West.

—◆—

Jane had a choice to make. She could stop in Nauvoo,

or

she could never give up following her faith.

Jane was unstoppable in her faith and chose to go west with the Saints. She walked another thousand miles to Utah. As she crossed the plains, Jane gave birth to her second son, waded through streams, searched for food, and fought dust storms, but she would not give up. The unstoppable Jane was one of the first pioneers to settle in the Salt Lake Valley in 1847. Her hardships did not end there, but she never gave up. Jane was a member of the Church for over eighty years and said,

"My faith in the gospel of Jesus Christ . . . is as strong today, nay, it is, if possible, stronger than it was the day I was first baptized."

Amen!

When have you chosen to be unstoppable in your faith?

EMMELINE B. WELLS
A Thinker

Emmeline was a thinker. When she was growing up, many girls in America were not able to get a formal education. But because of her active mind, she had the rare opportunity to study at an excellent school. Watching her widowed mother lead her family, Emmeline thought that girls could do anything. When Emmeline was introduced to the gospel, she discovered that the doctrines matched her ideas about women's potential. She knew Joseph Smith had been inspired when he said to the women of the Church, "I now turn the key to you in the name of God, and this Society shall rejoice, and knowledge and intelligence shall flow down from this time—this is the beginning of better days." Emmeline thought this was true. But not everyone agreed with her.

⊳—◇—⊴

Emmeline had a choice to make. She could be embarrassed by her ideas,

or

she could trust that her ideas were true.

Emmeline chose to trust her thoughts. In a blessing, God told her, "You will live to do a work that has never been done by any woman since the Creation." Humbled by this revelation, Emmeline devoted her life to helping women reach their divine potential.

So . . . Emmeline lobbied presidents of the United States and visited the White House five times; she raised five faithful daughters; she advocated for women to hold political office; she organized women to save grain to feed the poor; she worked for almost four decades as the editor of the *Woman's Exponent*—a newspaper to spread women's voices; and she served as the General President of the Relief Society for eleven years. By thinking and trusting her ideas, Emmeline created a better day for women everywhere.

⁂

When have you acted on an inspired idea?

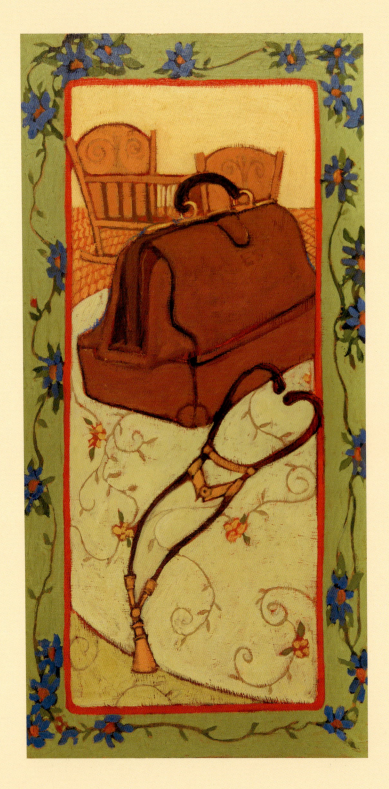

ᚠELLIS ᚠSHIPP
The Determined Doctor

Ellis was a determined woman. Settling the Utah territory in the 1860s, she and her husband wanted to have a family. She gave birth to ten children, but only six of them survived. Many babies died during childbirth because there were not enough skilled doctors and midwives to care for them. The death of so many children devastated Ellis.

⋯⋯⋯⋯◆⋯⋯⋯⋯

Ellis had a choice to make. She could mourn that too many babies were dying,

or

she could do something to solve the problem.

Ellis chose to make things better. She knew childbirth was a gift from God, and she was determined to make it safer. Encouraged by her family and the prophet Brigham Young, Ellis moved all the way across the country to attend medical school. She became pregnant during her studies, but that did not deter her. Ellis prayed that she would still be able to complete her studies—and gave birth the day after her exams.

Ellis became one of the first female doctors in Utah. But she knew that one doctor couldn't solve such a big problem. So Dr. Ellis started a nursing school in Salt Lake City and taught more than five hundred midwives to safely deliver babies. Ellis was set apart by Apostles to be a midwife, and she used both her school knowledge and her spiritual knowledge to strengthen women in labor. During her fifty years as a doctor and midwife, Ellis welcomed over five thousand babies into the world. Balancing medicine and motherhood, she cared for her own family while saving lives in her community.

When have you been determined to solve a problem?

Desideria Quintanar de Yáñez
A Visionary Matriarch

Desideria was a visionary. A descendant of Cuauhtémoc—one of the last Aztec emperors—she was a strong, spiritual matriarch. Desideria lived on a hacienda near Nopala, Mexico, with her husband and three children. When Desideria was sixty-six years old, she had a dream about a booklet called *Voz de Amonestación* (*A Voice of Warning*). She was told in her dream that the booklet contained God's teachings and could be found in Mexico City. Desideria immediately wanted to get a copy of the booklet. But Mexico City was seventy-five miles away, and she was so sick she couldn't even walk. How could she travel there? Or roam the streets trying to find the booklet?

Desideria had a choice to make. She could ignore her dream,

or

she could believe her dream was a vision and search for the booklet.

Desideria chose to act on her vision. She sent her oldest son, José, to Mexico City to search for the booklet. José wandered the city asking strangers if anyone knew about *Voz de Amonestación*. After days and days of searching, José miraculously found the booklet! Some of the Church's first missionaries in Mexico were busy translating the booklet into Spanish. Nobody even had a copy yet.

When Desideria heard that the booklet from her vision existed, she was elated. She knew its teachings must be from God, and she wanted to be baptized. A few months later, a missionary traveled to her village and baptized Desideria and some of her family in the stream by their hacienda. They were among the first members of the Church in Mexico and received the first known copy of the Book of Mormon in Spanish. Even though there was never a ward in her community, Desideria remained enthusiastic about the gospel her whole life. Her vision had taught her an important truth: God was aware of her and her family.

———◇———

When have you chosen to act on a message from God?

Inez Knight and Jennie Brimhall
First Sister Missionaries

Inez and Jennie were eager! They had been exploring together ever since they were young girls. They grew up and decided to study at Brigham Young Academy. And soon after graduation, the wider world called. The friends planned a big trip to Europe to see the sights and visit Inez's two brothers serving missions.

However, God had an even better plan for Inez and Jennie. God inspired their bishop to invite them to serve missions too. The girls were shocked! There had never been single sister missionaries before. But times were changing. God was ready to call sister missionaries, knowing their powerful testimonies would open hearts. Paving the way for all future sister missionaries, the prophet Wilford Woodruff called Inez and Jennie to serve in England.

The friends had a choice to make. They could continue with their planned vacation,

or

they could accept the call to be the first single sister missionaries.

Inez and Jennie chose to follow God's plan for them. They were set apart as missionaries on April 1, 1898, and left the very next day for England. Missionary life was full of adventures—stopping strangers on the street, speaking to large crowds, and singing throughout the city. Often the crowds were very curious to hear women speak.

Sadly, after a few months, Jennie got sick and had to return home. But Inez continued to serve—sometimes alone—for over two years. Sister Inez traveled throughout England and Europe representing the Church and teaching God's plan. One time a crowd refused to listen to the elder missionaries but were willing to hear from her, a sister missionary. Trusting in God's plan, Jennie and Inez changed missionary work forever.

When have you chosen to follow God's plan for you?

Sarah M. Kimball, Emily F. Richards, and Mattie Hughes Cannon

Suffragist Saints

Sarah, Emily, and Mattie were a talented trio.

Sarah was an organizer. She believed that people could do big things if they came together. After attending the School of the Prophets, Sarah organized a charitable sewing group that quickly became the first Relief Society. Emily was an eloquent speaker. Whenever she expressed her beliefs, people listened. Emily served as a spokesperson for the Church and traveled the country giving speeches. Mattie was a change maker. She yearned to learn and use her knowledge for good. Mattie earned four degrees, in medicine, chemistry, pharmaceuticals, and oratory. Sometimes she was the only girl in her class.

Sarah, Emily, and Mattie were free to organize, speak, learn, and work. But they all lacked one important freedom—they were not free to vote!

———◆———

They had a choice to make. They could accept this injustice,

or

they could use their God-given talents to win the right to vote.

Sarah, Emily, and Mattie knew the Church endorsed the suffragist movement—so they decided to get to work.

Sarah chose to organize. She believed that the Relief Society would open up the way for women to win the right to vote. So she organized new Relief Society groups all over Utah, led the way in constructing new buildings for women to gather, and served as a Relief Society president for forty years.

Emily chose to speak. Her powerful speeches helped women in Utah win the right to vote—long before other women in the rest of the United States. But even after that victory, Emily kept speaking up. She worked for all women in America to be able to vote—and in 1920, they finally won!

Mattie chose to be a change maker. She ran for office and surprised everyone when she beat her husband in the election. Mattie became the first female state senator in the entire country! In her first month, Senator Mattie introduced three bills to help blind people, improve working conditions for women and girls, and keep people healthy.

This talented trio had won the right to vote and used that right to light the world.

⌐·····——◆——·····⌐

When have you used your talents to change the world for good?

References

Introduction

Russell M. Nelson, "Sisters' Participation in the Gathering of Israel," *Ensign*, November 2018.

Lucy Mack Smith: Mother Moses

Lucy Mack Smith, *History of Joseph Smith* (Salt Lake City: Bookcraft, 1958), 203–4.

Emma Hale Smith: An Extraordinary Leader

Emma Smith, in Relief Society Minute Book, Nauvoo, Illinois, March 17, 1842, Church History Library, 12.

Eliza R. Snow: Zion's Poetess

Eliza R. Snow, "My Father in Heaven," in "Poetry, for the Times and Seasons," *Times and Seasons* 6 (November 15, 1845): 1039; see also "O My Father," *Hymns*, no. 292.

Zina Young: The Great Mother Heart

Zina D. H. Young, in Brittany Chapman Nash and Richard E. Turley Jr., eds., *Women of Faith in the Latter Days*, Volume 4 (Salt Lake City: Deseret Book, 2017), 135–36.

Jane Manning James: The Unstoppable Pioneer

Linda King Newell and Valeen Tippetts Avery, "Jane Manning James: Black Saint, 1847 Pioneer," *Ensign*, August 1979.

Jane E. Manning James, "My Life Story," as dictated to Elizabeth J. D. Roundy, Wilford Woodruff Papers, Historical Department, The Church of Jesus Christ of Latter-day Saints, Salt Lake City, Utah.

Emmeline B. Wells: A Thinker

Joseph Smith, in Relief Society Minute Book, Nauvoo, Illinois, April 28, 1842, 40.

Relief Society Magazine 2 (February 1915): 47.